Mullah Nasruddin

In Istanbul

by

Mansoor Shah

Manchester
U. K.

2014

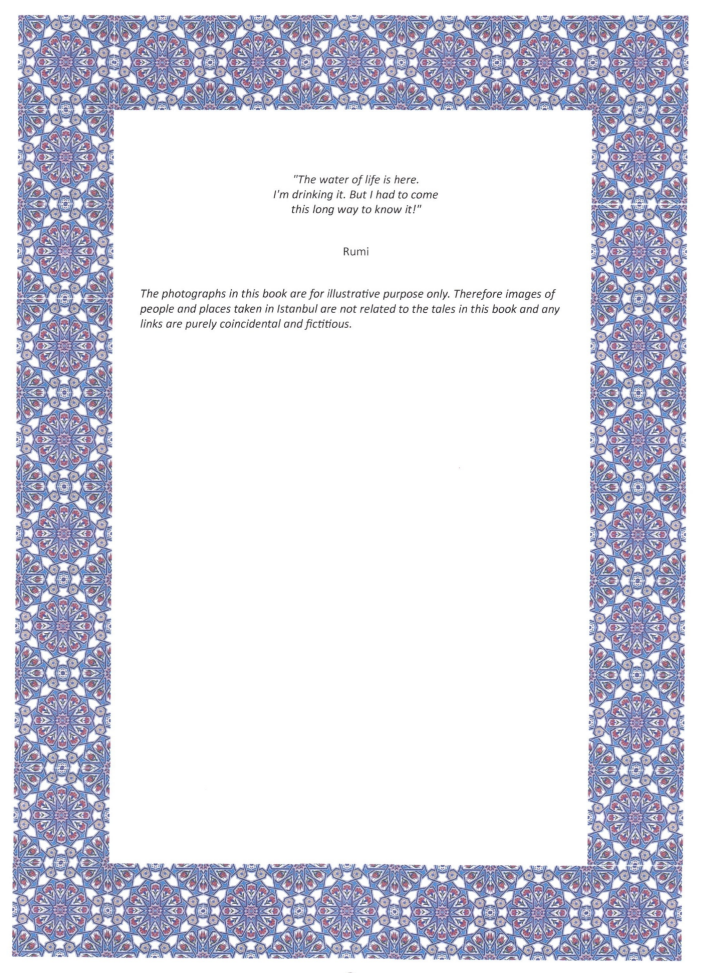

*"The water of life is here.
I'm drinking it. But I had to come
this long way to know it!"*

Rumi

The photographs in this book are for illustrative purpose only. Therefore images of people and places taken in Istanbul are not related to the tales in this book and any links are purely coincidental and fictitious.

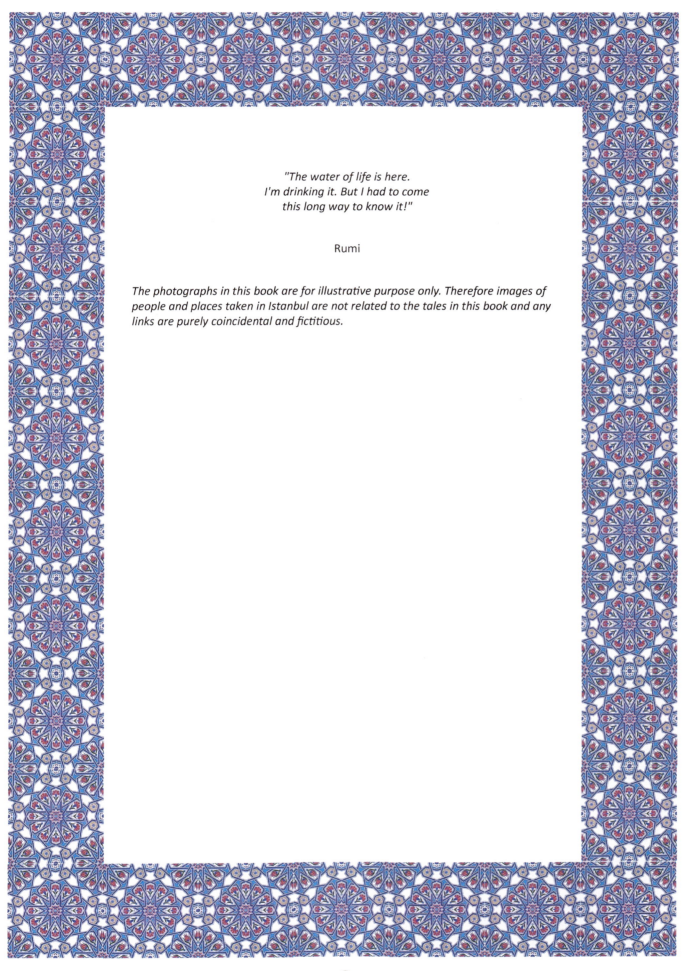

"The water of life is here.
I'm drinking it. But I had to come
this long way to know it!"

Rumi

The photographs in this book are for illustrative purpose only. Therefore images of people and places taken in Istanbul are not related to the tales in this book and any links are purely coincidental and fictitious.

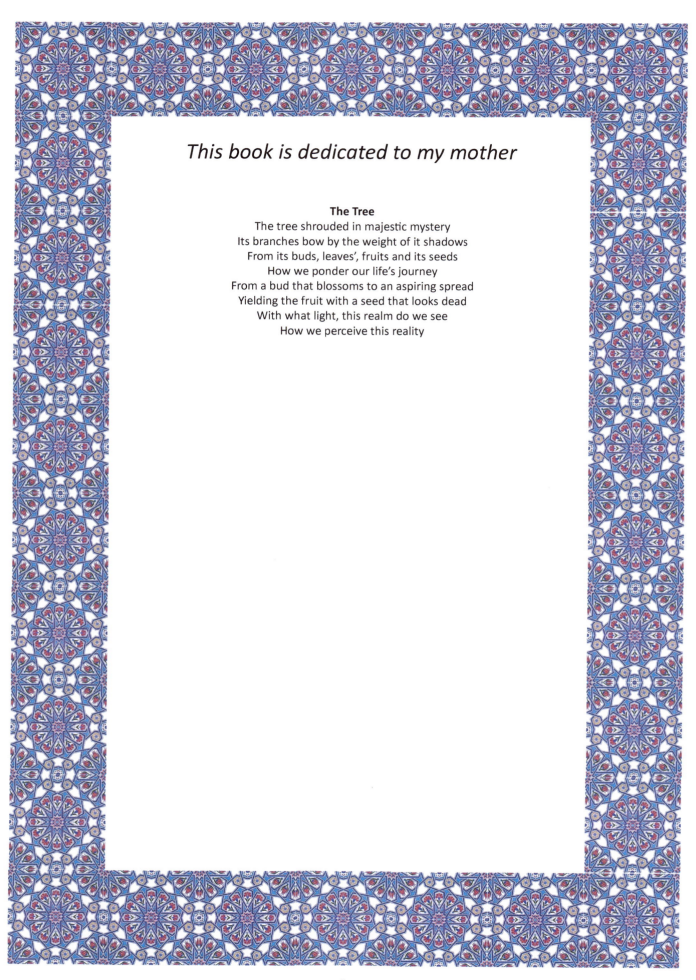

This book is dedicated to my mother

The Tree
The tree shrouded in majestic mystery
Its branches bow by the weight of it shadows
From its buds, leaves', fruits and its seeds
How we ponder our life's journey
From a bud that blossoms to an aspiring spread
Yielding the fruit with a seed that looks dead
With what light, this realm do we see
How we perceive this reality

5

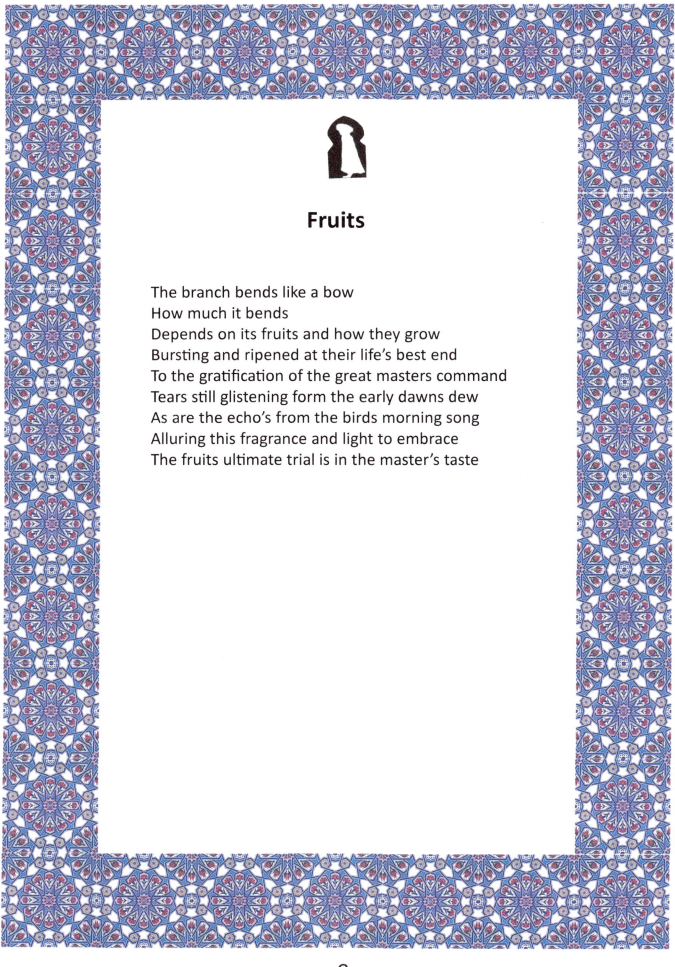

Fruits

The branch bends like a bow
How much it bends
Depends on its fruits and how they grow
Bursting and ripened at their life's best end
To the gratification of the great masters command
Tears still glistening form the early dawns dew
As are the echo's from the birds morning song
Alluring this fragrance and light to embrace
The fruits ultimate trial is in the master's taste

CONTENTS

CONTENTS

CONTENTS

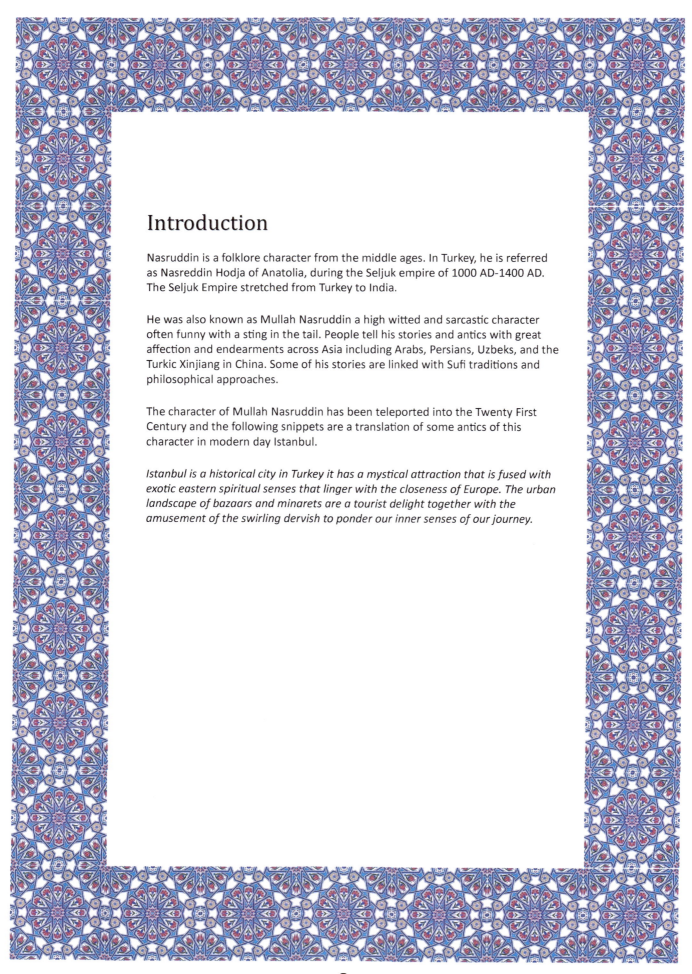

Introduction

Nasruddin is a folklore character from the middle ages. In Turkey, he is referred as Nasreddin Hodja of Anatolia, during the Seljuk empire of 1000 AD-1400 AD. The Seljuk Empire stretched from Turkey to India.

He was also known as Mullah Nasruddin a high witted and sarcastic character often funny with a sting in the tail. People tell his stories and antics with great affection and endearments across Asia including Arabs, Persians, Uzbeks, and the Turkic Xinjiang in China. Some of his stories are linked with Sufi traditions and philosophical approaches.

The character of Mullah Nasruddin has been teleported into the Twenty First Century and the following snippets are a translation of some antics of this character in modern day Istanbul.

Istanbul is a historical city in Turkey it has a mystical attraction that is fused with exotic eastern spiritual senses that linger with the closeness of Europe. The urban landscape of bazaars and minarets are a tourist delight together with the amusement of the swirling dervish to ponder our inner senses of our journey.

Quiet Room

Mullah Nasruddin's asked for a quiet room, as he was a light sleeper.
I will give you a quite room facing the Bosporus replied the hotel receptionist.
Are you sure its quiet stated Mullah Nasruddin.
Quite sure as I have not heard a word from that room chuckled the receptionist.
I assume your other rooms are talkative like you!
Retorted Mullah Nasruddin.

Room with a view

Mullah Nasruddin's checked into his room and the porter carried his luggage. The porter said, you know sir this is my favourite room in this hotel it has one of the best views. Mulla Nasruddin looked out of the window, yes I can see good views of the city and the Bosporus, but my best view is the Kiblah, What do you mean replied the porter.
You see what you want to see and I will see what I want to see explained the Mullah.

Directions to Topkapi Place

Mullah Nasruddin asked the directions to
Topkapi Palace from a street seller.
Do you really want to go there, the queues
are really long advised the street seller.
Just go through this archway and you will see
a line of tourists, then join the queue
sniggered the street seller.
Just because I asked you for the direction do
not assume that I will be going there but you
can rightly assume I will not be buying
anything from you replied
Mullah Nasruddin.

Images

Fortune Teller

Mullah Nasruddin spotted a man with a rooster and three rabbits professing to predict fortunes. He uses these animals to help him with his predictions.
Mulla Nasruddin's friend went to this fortune-teller. When he came back he seemed very upset. Mulla Nasruddin asked him, "What was the matter?" he said, "that fortune teller has said a few things and now I am very worried."
Mulla Nasruddin said, "Don't be worried. Nothing is certain in life so no prediction can be made. I tell you that only fools are certain."
His friend replied, "Are you really certain about that?"
He said, "Absolutely certain!"

Sultans Harem

Mullah Nasruddin was visiting the Harem in Topkapi Palace.
The security guard told the Mullah about the Sultans Harem
and how the Eunuchs always guarded this section.
Mullah Nasruddin said, I did not realise that you are a
Eunuch!
Mullah Nasruddin did not notice that the guard was about
to throw him out.

Sultans Treasures

Mullah Nasruddin was viewing the gifts, medals and diamond studded objects that were displayed at Topkapi Palace.

Another visitor remarked you see how rich and powerful these Sultans were.

Yes and the emphasis should be on the past and what they thought of themselves remarked the Mullah , in any case my treasures are far better than theirs.

The visitor looked at the Mullah up and down said are you being funny?

Mullah Nasrudin replied No just stating the obvious!

But I can't see your treasures questioned the visitor.

Exactly replied the Mullah
They are too precious to be displayed!

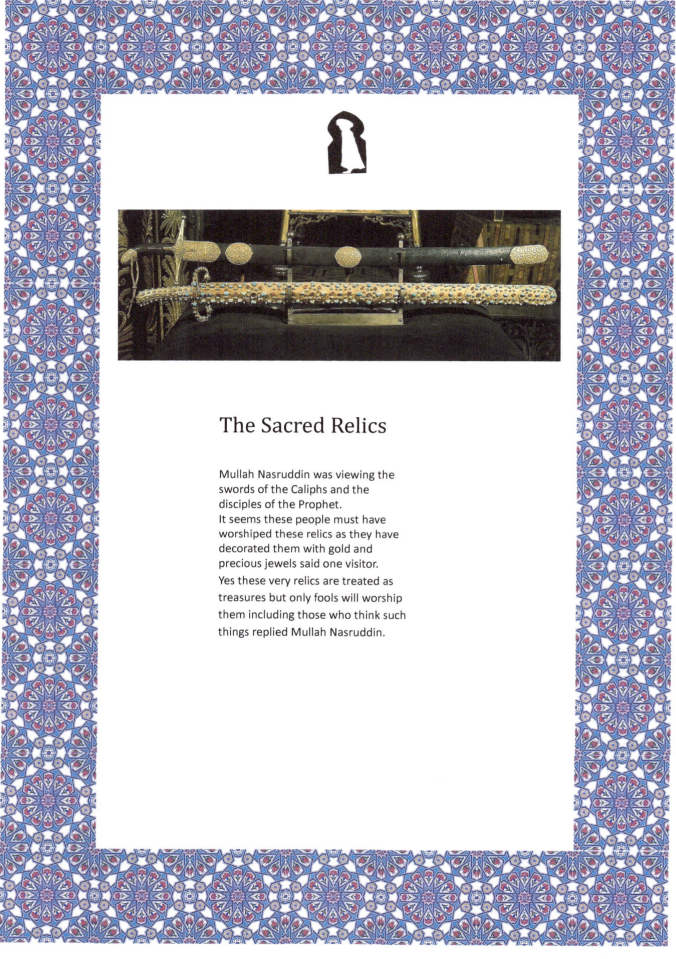

The Sacred Relics

Mullah Nasruddin was viewing the swords of the Caliphs and the disciples of the Prophet.
It seems these people must have worshiped these relics as they have decorated them with gold and precious jewels said one visitor.
Yes these very relics are treated as treasures but only fools will worship them including those who think such things replied Mullah Nasruddin.

Cheap Signage

Mullah Nasruddin spotted a long queue of women just outside the Harem entrance inside the Topkapi Palace.

That must be an interesting attraction said the Mullah, why is it only women who are queuing?

They are queuing to use the washrooms replied the women guard, that place is out of bounds to you.

So why are you guarding it replied Mullah Nasruddin.

To stop people like you getting in shouted the guard.

So where does it say women only questioned Mullah Nasruddin

It does not that is why I am here.

You must be a cheap sign replied Mullah Nasruddin

Trust

You fear losing a certain eminent position.
You hope to gain something from that,
but it comes from elsewhere.
Existence does this switching trick,
giving you hope from one source,
then satisfaction from another.
It keeps you bewildered and wondering,
and lets your trust in the unseen grow.

Rumi

Cable Cars

During a day trip to Pierre Loti Mullah
Nasruddin made some new few friends and
came across the entrance of the cable cars.
Nasruddin was asked about his opinion on the
safety of the cable cars.

He answered of course they are safe just
because they go over a large cemetery it does
not mean you will end up down there !

Real Way

"If I had known the real way it was,
I would have stopped all the looking around."
Rumi

Missing Seed

A passerby observed that Mullah Nasruddin was very busy searching the ground. She asked the Mullah had he lost something.
Mullah Nasruddin replied I buried a seed here a month ago but I can't find it. Maybe it grew into a plant and an animal has eaten it said the inquisitive woman. It was not that sort of seed replied the Mullah it was a spare bead for my tasbeh I put it here for safe keeping. Did you mark the spot said the woman. Of course I did it was directly under the shadow of a cloud but the cloud has disappeared and now I can't find it!!! Then you should wait until that cloud returns sniggered the woman!

Young Sultan

Mullah Nasruddin was visiting Eyup Sultan Mosque and he came across a family that were celebrating their son's circumcision, they had dressed him up as a Sultan. They offered Mullah Nasruddin a Turkish delight. The Mullah gave the boy some money; he said it is for the humiliation your parents are putting you through by dressing you up as a Sultan who gets the final chop!!!

The Tree & the Guide

The guide: "According to our records, this tree was here before the mosque was built it is nine hundred years old."
Nasrudin: "No—it's not, it's nine hundred and five years old."
" Well a couple years out its no big deal? Said the guide"
"You told me that this tree was nine hundred years old five years ago! So you probably lie about your age as well!"
Replied Mullah Nasruddin

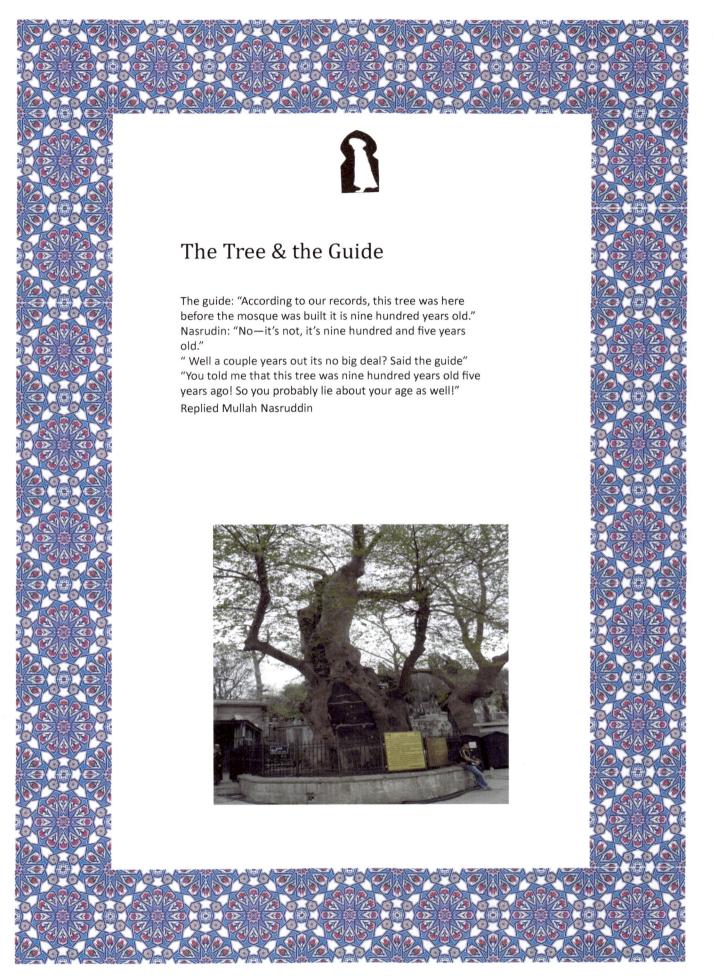

Pomegranate Juice Seller

Mullah Nasruddin saw a cart loaded with large pomegranates.
Are these pomegranates sweet and ripe questioned Nasruddin.
My pomegranates are excellent and juicy said the seller.
In that case I would like to try it first said Nasruddin .
The seller cut a few pomegranates and squeezed them into a juice and gave a glass to the Nasruddin.
Nasruddin quickly drank it, said you are right they are sweet and ripe and walked off.
But you have not paid me said the seller.
I did say that I would try it I did not say I would buy it replied the satisfied Nasruddin.

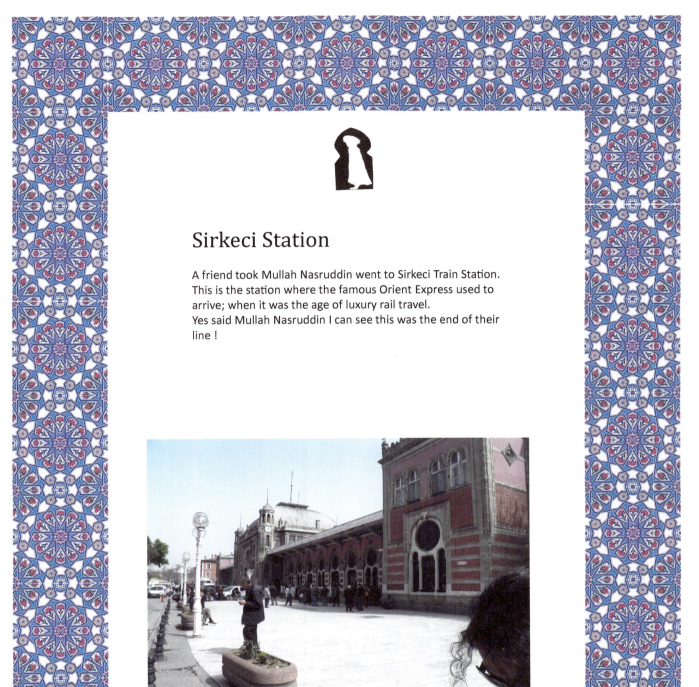

Sirkeci Station

A friend took Mullah Nasruddin went to Sirkeci Train Station.
This is the station where the famous Orient Express used to
arrive; when it was the age of luxury rail travel.
Yes said Mullah Nasruddin I can see this was the end of their
line !

Train to Ankra

Mullah Nasruddin bought a second-class train ticket to Ankra as the cost of a first class ticket was nearly twice as much? He noticed his friend bought a first -class ticket.

He said to his friend you know the difference you have paid for your ticket you could have fed so many poor people, do you not worry about your final destination.

His friend replied yes it is a worry.

I tell you what said Mullah Nasruddin, swap me your ticket and I will do the worrying for you!

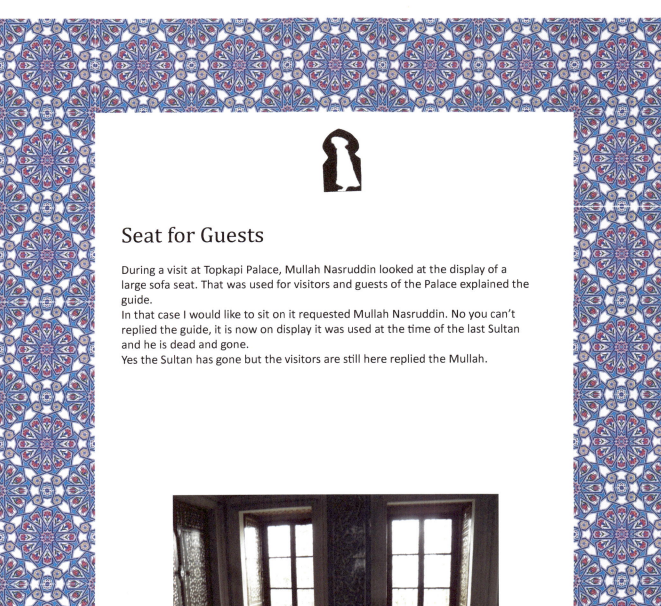

Seat for Guests

During a visit at Topkapi Palace, Mullah Nasruddin looked at the display of a large sofa seat. That was used for visitors and guests of the Palace explained the guide.

In that case I would like to sit on it requested Mullah Nasruddin. No you can't replied the guide, it is now on display it was used at the time of the last Sultan and he is dead and gone.

Yes the Sultan has gone but the visitors are still here replied the Mullah.

Suspension Bridge

Mullah Nasruddin was on a boat approaching the Bosporus Bridge. His friend said just imagine the engineering involved in making this bridge. Yes I am imagining it, now what do you want me to do? . Replied the Mullah. Just appreciate it said his friend.
Yes I can see how it is suspended, but look at the sky above it is Held up without any pillars do you imagine that!
Retorted Mullah Nasruddin.

The Leather Shop

Mullah Nasruddin wanted to buy a leather jacket.
How much is this jacket he asked the shopkeeper.
5000 Lira's answered the shopkeeper; I will give you 1000 Lira's for it said Nasruddin.
Sorry that is not possible make me a better offer said the shopkeeper. Ok guess how old I am and if you guess right I will buy it from you at the asking price. The shopkeeper looked at the Mullah and said Ok I bet you I am older than you, if you are older than me you can have the jacket for 1000 Lira's.
Deal said Nasruddin, and they shook their hands. The Shopkeeper showed his identity card with the proof of his age, Mullah Nasruddin smiled and showed that he was older by ten years at the dismay of the shop keeper .You don't look that old said the shopkeeper. But you do answered Nasruddin and gave the shopkeeper 1000 Lira's.

Timekeeping

Mullah Nasruddin was on his way to a meeting when a man stopped him and asked for the time.
It's between midday and late afternoon answered Mullah Nasruddin.
Don't you have a watch asked the man?
No that's why my meeting is between midday and late afternoon.
Answered Mullah Nasruddin.

Hand knotted carpets

Mullah Nasruddin was in the Grand Bazar buying a carpet. The carpet salesman was showing him a wide range of handmade carpets. He explained to Mullah Nasruddin that Hand knotted carpets were made of pure wool as opposed to factory carpets that were chemically processed and dyed materials. He further explained that hand knotted Turkish carpets involve a team of three or four weavers and each weavers size of knot will differ that is why the sizes are irregular. Whereas factory carpets are made by machines and mass-produced. He further explained that hand knotted carpets were unique, more appealing and were also a good investment. He said that he also has hand made silk carpets but they were too expensive for him.

Mullah Nasruddin felt patronised and said I am interested in a flying carpet, the one like Aladdin's. Ah replied the carpet salesman you need Aladdin's lamp for that.

If I had his lamp I would not be here listening to your sales patter retorted Mullah Nasruddin and walked off.

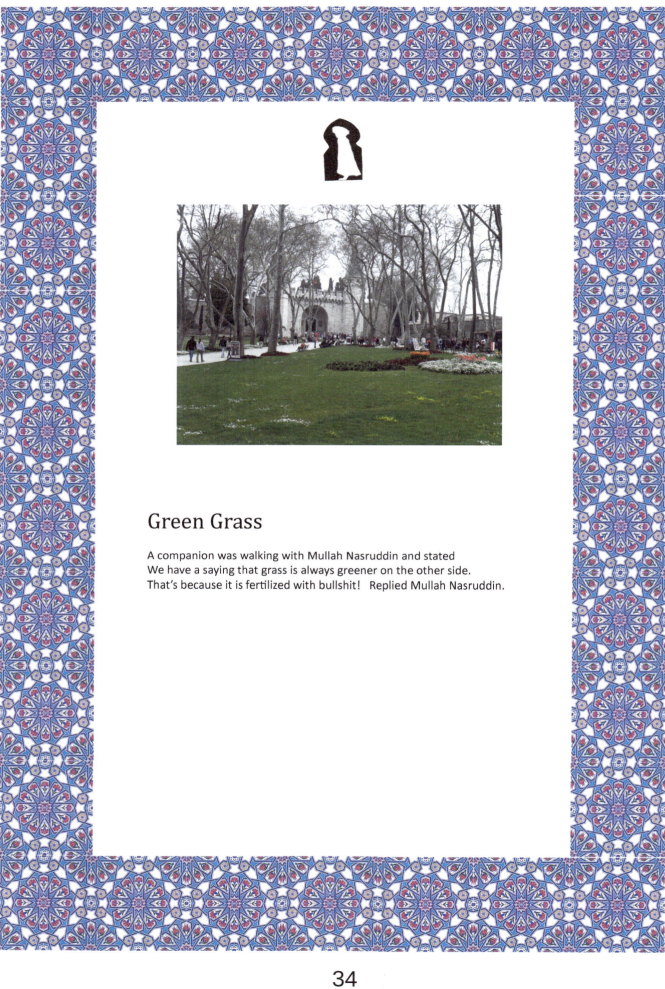

Green Grass

A companion was walking with Mullah Nasruddin and stated
We have a saying that grass is always greener on the other side.
That's because it is fertilized with bullshit!   Replied Mullah Nasruddin.

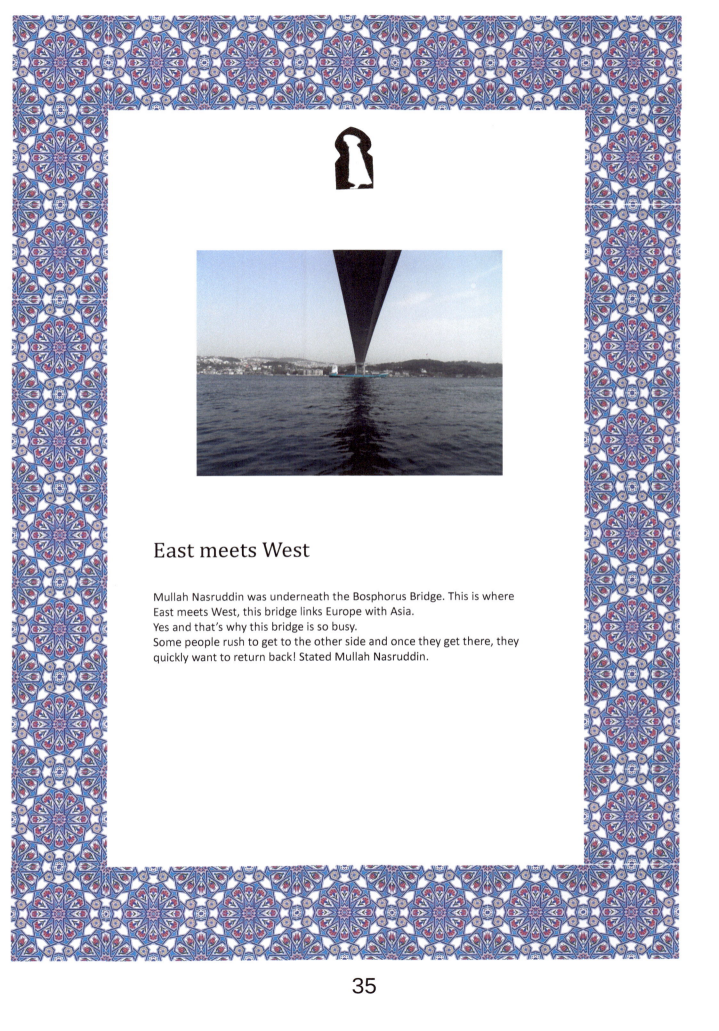

East meets West

Mullah Nasruddin was underneath the Bosphorus Bridge. This is where East meets West, this bridge links Europe with Asia.
Yes and that's why this bridge is so busy.
Some people rush to get to the other side and once they get there, they quickly want to return back! Stated Mullah Nasruddin.

Pretzels Seller

Mullah Nasruddin asked the pretzel seller how fresh were his pretzels.
They were baked this morning replied the seller.
They don't look that fresh queried Mullah Nasruddin.
Try one offered the seller.
Mullah Nasruddin ate it quickly.
Yes I was right it was not that fresh.
Aren't you going to pay for the one you have just ate the pretzel sell asked Mullah Nasruddin.
Of course not you offered me to try it not to buy it.
Answered the smirked Mullah Nasruddin.

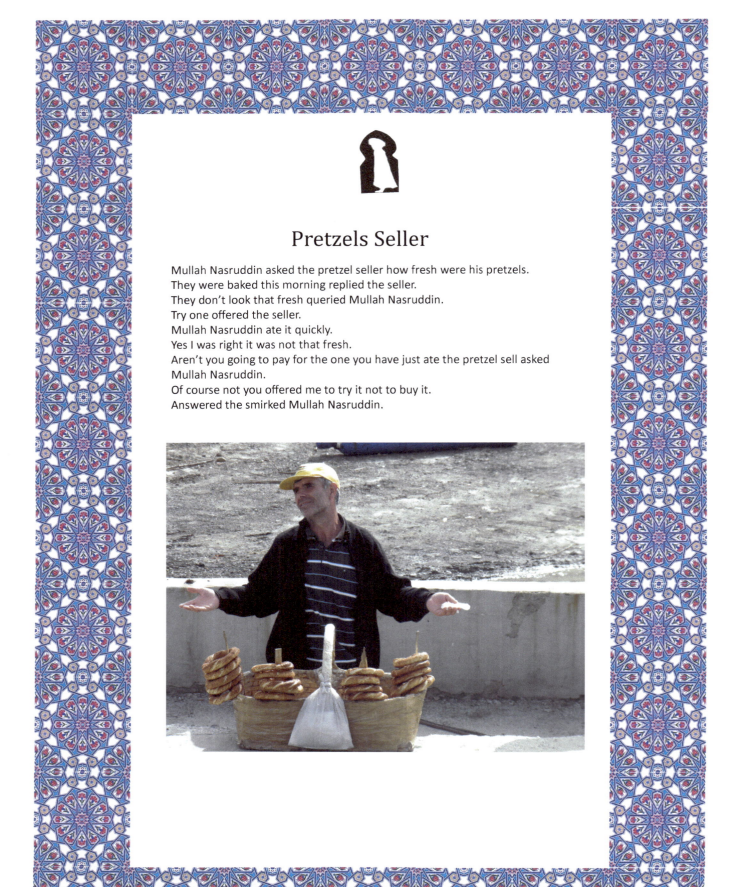

Worried Woman

Mullah Nasruddin was on a boat on the Bosporus. A woman who was sat opposite looked worried.

He told her have no fear all humans are like a few drops of water with a thousand anxieties.

She said I can cope with the anxieties it's the thousand drops of water I am worried about!

Istanbul Taxi Driver

Mullah Nasruddin was getting a lift in a taxi; the driver boasted how knowledgeable the taxi drivers were in Istanbul they knew even the potholes in every street.

Yes just like my donkey I am guided by his tail said Mullah Nasruddin.

What do you mean said the puzzled taxi driver?

I just sit on its back facing the tail and the donkey takes me in the opposite direction.

Why don't you sit facing forward questioned the taxi driver.

I do not like potholes! Stated Mullah Nasruddin.

Swirling Dervish

Mullah Nasruddin was walking with his friend when they passed a poster advertising the swirling dervishes.
Mullah Nasruddin told his friend that he used to do that. When he swirled the spectators disappeared.
His friend said really were you swirling that fast!
No replied Mullah Nasruddin they walked away disappointed.

Shadow

The enjoyment of this life
Is like thy shadow.
If you stop.
It stops:
Try to overtake it,
It moves on.

Maxims of Ali

Water Cannon

Mullah Nasruddin spotted police and a water cannon.
His friend advised Mullah Nasruddin to leave the area, as there could be trouble.
They are just dampening the streets; it's not their fault if a few people get in their way!
Yes I am sure you won't complain when you get drenched and bruised explained his friend.
That will not happen because you will be in front of me replied Mullah Nasruddin

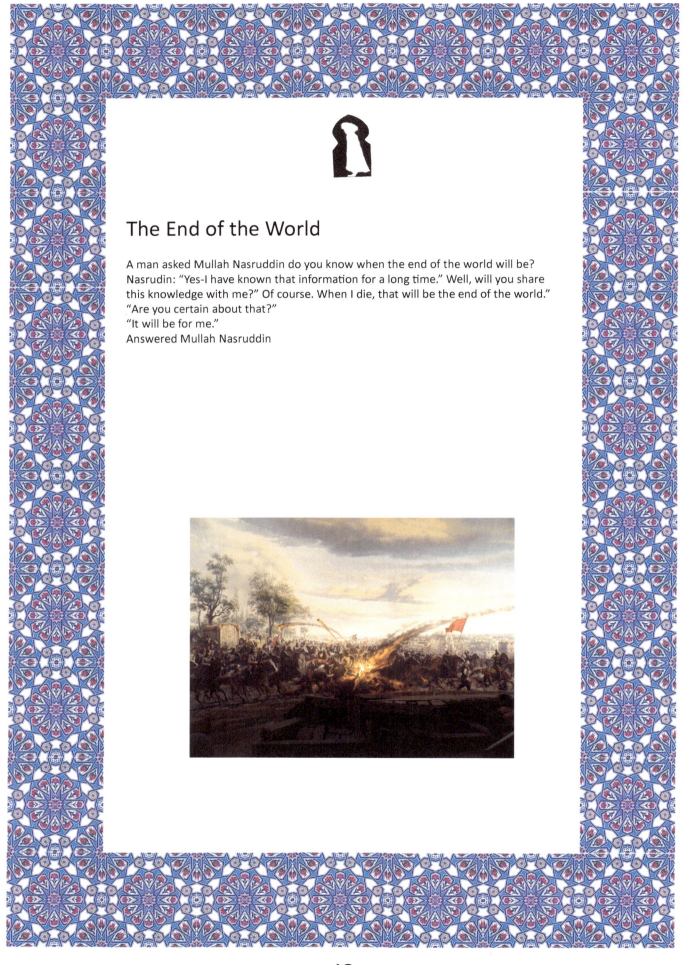

The End of the World

A man asked Mullah Nasruddin do you know when the end of the world will be?
Nasrudin: "Yes-I have known that information for a long time." Well, will you share
this knowledge with me?" Of course. When I die, that will be the end of the world."
"Are you certain about that?"
"It will be for me."
Answered Mullah Nasruddin

Bosporus Tourists

These boats are very popular with the tourist announced a companion of Mullah Nasruddin.
So why is this one is nearly empty stated Mullah Nasruddin.
Perhaps this one is on a private tour replied the companion.
What is so private about them, when they are displaying their arrogance in public? Stated Mullah Nasruddin.

The Intelligent Man

The intelligent man is whoever knows
How to be happier today than yesterday!

Maxims of Ali

Famous Sheikh

An old woman accidentally bumped into a sheikh who was walking past. Mullah Nasruddin said to her "do you know who this sheikh is that you have just bumped into." "No", replied the old woman. Well-replied Mullah Nasruddin he has written many books about thousands of reasons why Allah exists. The old woman then stated that he must have had 'thousands of doubts about Allah's existence!' Immediately Mullah Nasruddin told the sheikh what this old woman had just stated. The sheikh upon hearing this dropped to his knees and prayed " Oh Allah please accept my prayers as you accept this old woman's prayers"

Deceptive Rules

Mullah Nasruddin was asked if he would be happy if a country was ruled by religion.
Certainly not answered the Mullah,there are two types of religions:
One: Where God has ordained the heavens and earth sending his messengers to proclaim his ownership of infinite governance.

The other: Ignorant men and women conjecturing a domination of deceptive rules!

Istanbul

A city of colour and exotic treats
Hidden cherishes unveiling the pleasing eye
Amongst the noise of its clamoured streets
The minarets spring up like darts fired into the sky
Echoing the time of its journeys past
Scents linger and embrace its curios passers by
With gifts of remembrance to ever last
This great city on Bosporus Shores as it parts
The West from East & its cultural arts
Like a rose in a desert that is admired
An oasis of a mirage desired as its ramparts
From the Pretzel seller to the Shoe Shine Man's shouts
The carpet seller and the lanterns light
This is Istanbul's Turkish delight

Zero to One

Starts from zero and end at one
Some end when it really has begun
Some seem to have a very short deed
Some want to extend along with greed
All follow different paths and often astray
All leading to a destination and the final day
With dear ones and those that are cared
Parts of this is lovingly shared
Some will leave their mark or stain
Mark of a reward or a mark of pain
Some follow difficulty without stealth
Others follow the deception of wealth
Leading to an exit or gate that is strong
The measure of deeds of right and wrong
Playing out choices as you were warned
You already know what you have earned
This final submission has now receded
Zero to one that is all what was need
Master of the keys has always succeeded

Water Seller

A man offered some water to Mullah Nasruddin. You remind me of a man who had a dream about drinking water. The water seller wanted to know more and asked the Mullah to explain.Well replied Mullah Nasruddin this man told everyone not to drink water from their well in the village as it would make them mad.He told them to drink the water from another source but they refused to believe him.Sure enough they started to act strange they would not talk to him and behaved very differently towards him.See I did warn you that you all would go mad if you drank the water from that well. Some months passed and this man now had ran out of his supply of water and had no choice but to drink from the same well.As soon as he drank it he was the same as everyone else and they accepted him as one of their own!
Does that mean you will buy my water said the water seller ? Certainly not! I do not want to be as mad as you! answered Mullah Nasruddin

Mullah Nasruddin

Are you sure that was Mullah Nasruddin?

Of course I am sure, do you know anyone else in Istanbul that is as slow to take out his purse and fastest to put it back in his pocket!